Ndebele Beadwork: African Artistry

Ann Stalcup

The Rosen Publishing Group's
PowerKids Press™
New York

To my husband, Ed, who shares my love of folk art and travel

Special thanks to Gary van Wyk.

Published in 1999 by The Rosen Publishing Group, Inc.
29 East 21st Street, New York, NY 10010

Copyright © 1999 by The Rosen Publishing Group, Inc.

First Edition

Book Design: Resa Listort

Photo Credits: pp. 4, 7, 8, 9, 10, 11, 12, 13, 14, 15, 16, 18, 19 by Elizabeth A. Schneider; pp. 20–21 by Christine Inramorato.

Stalcup, Ann, 1935-
    Ndebele beadwork: African artistry / by Ann Stalcup.
        p. cm. — (Crafts of the world)
    Includes index.
    Summary: Focuses on the importance of beadwork in the lives of Africa's Ndebele people. Includes instructions for making an Ndebele doll.
    ISBN 0-8239-5336-X
    1. Beadwork, Nguni—Juvenile literature. 2. Ndebele (African people)—Juvenile literature. [1. Ndbele (African people). 2. Beadwork. 3. Handicraft.]
I. Title. II. Series.
DT2913.N44S73 1998
745.58'2'089963977—dc21

98-3878
CIP
AC

Manufactured in the United States of America

Contents

Who Are the Ndebele?

The **Ndebele** (en-DEH-beh-leh) are a people who live in South Africa. The Ndebele are famous for their colorful art. Their houses are painted with bright **geometric** (jee-oh-MEH-trik) designs. Their **traditional** (truh-DIH-shuh-nul) costumes are decorated with many brightly colored beads. The **beadwork** (BEED-werk) and paintings are all made by Ndebele women. The Ndebele women are proud of their art. Art is one way to show how important a woman is in her community. Some women earn money by selling their beadwork. Others have become famous all around the world for their painting.

◀ This is a traditionally painted Ndebele homestead, or home.

Ndebele Costumes

For many years, the Ndebele have worn the same kind of clothing that you and I wear. But on special occasions they wear traditional costumes. The costumes show that they are very proud of their **culture** (KUL-cher) and **heritage** (HEHR-ih-tij).

Ndebele women wear metal neck and leg rings and beaded headpieces, collars, blankets, and aprons. Different styles of beaded aprons are worn for different reasons, and at different times in a woman's life. For her wedding an Ndebele bride wears a long, goatskin **cloak** (KLOHK), called a *linaga* (lee-NAH-gah). Some *linaga* are heavily beaded and can weigh up to 50 pounds! Today women often wear beaded blankets instead.

The Ndebele save their
fine costumes for special
occasions. ▶

Beading

Ndebele women may spend their spare time sorting, stringing, and stitching beads. Ndebele girls watch carefully to learn how to make beadwork and paint designs. Girls are taught beadwork and painting by their mothers, grandmothers, and aunts.

Until the late 1950s, the beads that the Ndebele used were mainly white. Now colorful glass beads are sold at local trading stores. The Ndebele use many colors and patterns in their costumes today.

Once, beads were sewn onto leather or cloth with animal **sinew** (SIN-yoo). But today Ndebele women use strong thread. Even though the **materials** (muh-TEER-ee-ulz) used today make the work easier, beading still takes time, patience, and skill.

Many colored beads are available for the Ndebele to use.
◄ Some of these colored beads come from the Czech Republic in Europe.

9

Ndebele Children

Ndebele children wear beads before they wear clothes. Soon after babies are born, they wear white beads around their waists. This is supposed to bring good luck. As the babies get older, they wear beads around their ankles, wrists, and necks. Young girls wear a fringed **loincloth** (LOYN-kloth) called a *ghabi*.

Like most Ndebele children, this girl will wear beads before she wears her first apron.

Ndebele children wear uniforms to school. But they wear traditional costumes for special occasions and **ceremonies** (SEHR-ih-moh-neez). Each child wears the same type of beaded clothing. But the colors and designs on their clothing are very different from one another.

This young girl wears a colorful *ghabi.* ▶

Beaded Aprons

After a girl turns fourteen years old, she wears a stiff, rectangular apron called a *phephetu* (peh-PEH-too).

Different styles of aprons mean different things. Brides wear a *liphoto* (lee-POH-toh), which is an apron that has two square flaps with a beaded fringe in between. After a woman has her first child she may wear an *ijogolo* (ee-JOH-goh-loh), an apron with five rounded panels.

Aprons used to be made out of goatskin. Today, goatskin is used only for special aprons. Everyday aprons are made out of cheaper materials, such as plastic.

◀ These two women are wearing *liphotos*.

Headbands and Neckpieces

The **headdresses** (HED-dres-ez) and headbands worn by Ndebele women for special occasions are very **ornate** (or-NAYT). Long beaded strips that touch the floor hang down each side of the headdress. Some headdresses are very tall.

When they are fully dressed, Ndebele women look different from the women of other African peoples.

14

Mirrors, plastic watches, and tin butterflies are sometimes attached for decoration.

After marriage, a woman wears neck rings. In the past rings were made of copper. But today most Ndebele women wear plastic rings. Women also wear big, colorful, rope-like neck collars.

The costumes of older Ndebele women are always the most colorful and ornate. ▶

Ceremonies

Weddings are one of the most important ceremonies that the Ndebele celebrate. Often, Ndebele brides have a **Western-style** (WES-tern-STYL) wedding in the morning. Then they wear beautifully beaded **ceremonial** (sehr-ih-MOH-nee-ul) clothing for a traditional wedding in the afternoon. At the traditional ceremony the bride carries a foot-long wedding or dance stick. It is covered with beads and it has a knob at one end.

As teenagers, both boys and girls have special ceremonies called **initiations** (ih-nih-shee-AY-shunz). They are times of great celebration. Once initiated, boys and girls are treated as young men and women. At their initiations, both boys and girls are given beaded gifts.

The beaded veil that this bride wears is also an Ndebele tradition.

Dolls

Ndebele women make dolls for themselves and their children. They sell the dolls too. Today, Ndebele dolls can be seen in books, and are found in folk-art shops all around the world.

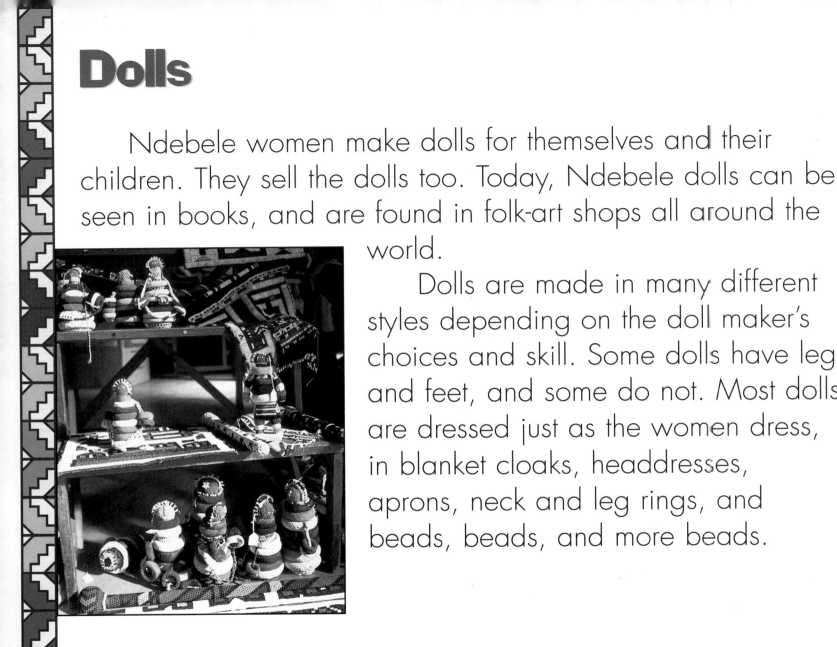

Dolls are made in many different styles depending on the doll maker's choices and skill. Some dolls have legs and feet, and some do not. Most dolls are dressed just as the women dress, in blanket cloaks, headdresses, aprons, neck and leg rings, and beads, beads, and more beads.

Many people who visit the Ndebele buy beaded dolls to bring home with them.

Doll Making:

You will need:

1 cardboard toilet paper roll
construction paper (any colors)
1 pipe cleaner
beads of any color
markers

circle of tissue paper, 8 inches
   across, any color
about 18 strands of yarn in 10-inch
   strips
cotton balls

rubber band
glue
scissors
one pin

First, let's make the doll's head:

1. Put the cotton balls on the tissue paper and gather the ends of paper together with the rubber band.

2. Glue the yarn onto the head for the hair.

3. Draw a face with the markers.

20

Now let's make the clothing:

1. Cut two pieces of construction paper: one 2 x 2 ½ inches, the other 5 x 7 inches

2. Decorate both pieces of construction paper by drawing simple shapes with the glue. Gently pour beads over the glue designs.

3. Let the beads sit for about 10 minutes. Pour any loose beads back into their container. Let the designs dry for about 40 minutes.

4. Glue the smaller piece of paper to the front of the toilet paper roll. This is the doll's apron.

5. Wrap the larger piece of construction paper around the roll and push the pin through the paper and the roll.

6. Place the head on top of the toilet paper roll.

7. Wrap the pipe cleaner around the neck of the doll.

21

The Ndebele Way of Life

Today many Ndebele live in cities. Their lives are very much like the lives of people who live in cities in other parts of the world. But the Ndebele who live on farms are different. They follow Ndebele traditions.

Ndebele houses on the farms are simple. They have no telephones or TVs. But TVs are often painted on the walls of homes, along with lightbulbs and airplanes! The Ndebele have seen these items, and paint them, even though they are not part of Ndebele life on the farms.

Ndbele women have many **responsibilities** (reh-spon-sih-BIH-lih-teez) on the farms. They plant crops and tend to farm animals. The Ndebele are most proud of keeping their houses freshly painted and creating beadwork for others to see.

Glossary

beadwork (BEED-werk) Beautiful designs created using beads.

ceremonial (sehr-ih-MOH-nee-ul) Having to do with a ceremony.

ceremony (SEHR-ih-moh-nee) A special series of acts that are done on certain occasions.

cloak (KLOHK) A heavy, blanket-like cloth worn around the shoulders.

culture (KUL-cher) The beliefs, customs, art, and religion of a group of people.

geometric (jee-oh-MEH-trik) Having to do with lines, circles, squares, and triangles.

headdress (HED-dres) Something that is worn on the head.

heritage (HEHR-ih-tij) The cultural traditions that are handed down from parent to child.

ijogolo (ee-JOH-goh-loh) An apron with five rounded panels worn by women with children.

initiation (ih-nih-shee-AY-shun) A ceremony where someone becomes a member of a group, such as when a boy becomes a man or a girl becomes a woman.

linaga (lee-NAH-gah) A long, goatskin cloak worn by Ndebele brides.

liphoto (lee-POH-toh) An apron that has two square flaps with a beaded fringe between.

loincloth (LOYN-kloth) A small apron worn around the hips.

material (muh-TEER-ee-ul) The things needed to make something.

Ndebele (en-DEH-beh-leh) An African people who live in South Africa.

ornate (or-NAYT) Highly decorated.

phephetu (peh-PEH-too) A stiff, rectangular apron worn by girls after they turn fourteen.

responsibility (reh-spon-sih-BIH-lih-tee) Something, such as a chore, that a person must do.

sinew (SIN-yoo) A strong body tissue used as sewing thread.

traditional (truh-DIH-shuh-nul) The way people have done something for many years.

Western-style (VVES-tern-STYL) The style of people in the Western Hemisphere, such as Americans or Europeans.

Index